# The *Soul Care* Journal

with **50** DAILY WRITING PROMPTS TO ENGAGE YOUR MIND AND HEAL YOUR HEART

*Gabi Kelley*

Copyright 2021 Gabi Kelley

All rights reserved. No portion of this work may be reproduced in any form without prior consent of the creator.

Published by Kelley Creative.

ISBN 978-1-953625-12-0

kelley creative
SPOKANE · WA · USA

*H*ello beautiful!

*I am so glad you're here.*

Wherever you are, whoever you are, whatever you're facing, and however you're feeling, I want you to know that you belong here.

This journal was created from recognizing the need for people like me—trauma survivors, empaths, and dreamers—to have safe spaces to open their hearts and share their thoughts unedited. We face so many constraints to voicing our true feelings and thoughts and struggles in this world as we try to fit into the molds that society has for us. I wanted to cultivate an environment where we don't have to stay inside those molds, and where we can show up as our truly authentic selves.

*Because here's the thing . . .*

Your story matters. What's going on in your heart matters. Your feelings matter. And being able to openly and honestly assess what it happening inside of you can be a deeply healing experience.

I cannot wait for you to open this book and feel a sense of relief, knowing, "I can be myself here." These prompts are designed to tenderly open your heart to welcome healing in a safe space.

You are so worthwhile, my friend, and I am deeply grateful for you.

Much Joy,

*Gabi Kelley*

www.gabiruth.com | @gabiruth

# Day One

IMAGINE YOURSELF 5 YEARS IN THE FUTURE WAKING UP FROM A GOOD NIGHT'S SLEEP IN YOUR OWN BED. HOW DO YOU FEEL ABOUT YOUR LIFE IN THAT MOMENT?

Date:

# Day Two

*If you knew without a doubt in every fiber of your being that you were deeply, unconditionally, dearly loved... what would that feel like??*

Date:

# Day Three

DESCRIBE SOMETHING THAT IS GOING RIGHT IN YOUR LIFE RIGHT NOW.

Date:

# Day Four

Date:

# Day Five

*Imagine yourself in the most peaceful place in the world. What does it look, feel, smell, and sound like?*

Date:

# Day Six

What radical act of self care can you do today?

Date:

# Day Seven

What does growing older mean to you?

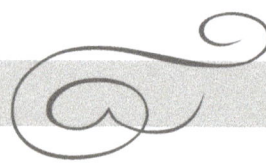

Date:

# Day Eight

Do you have a dream that scares you with its BIGness?? What is it?

# Day Nine

What is something you are excited about right now?

Date:

# Day Ten

How deeply do you believe that you matter and your story matters? Why do you feel that way?

Date:

# Day Eleven

Where does it hurt, sweetheart?

# Day Twelve

Describe your greatest accomplishment and why you're so proud of it.

Date:

# Day Thirteen

What parts of you are genuine? Which parts of you do you put on for show?

# Day Fourteen

*Who are the most supportive people in your world right now, and what makes them feel supportive?*

Date:

# Day Fifteen

Date:

# Day Sixteen

What opportunities have come your way recently that you are grateful for?

Date:

# Day Seventeen

What words of encouragement do you need today?

Date:

# Day Eighteen

Write about your first love, whether that be a person, place, or thing...

Date:

# Day Nineteen

What are you afraid to ask for when you're going through a hard time? Why is that ask scary for you?

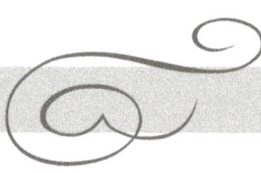

# Day Twenty

What's something you have that isn't expensive but that means a lot to you? What's the story behind it?

Date:

# Day Twenty-One

How do you treat yourself when you're not feeling well?

# Day Twenty-Two

You get to relive one experience from your life. Which one do you choose?

Date:

# Day Twenty-Three

What emotion is hardest for you to express? What steps can you take to gently help yourself be able to express that emotion?

Date:

# Day Twenty-Four

What is something that always works to boost your mood?

# Day Twenty-Five

What do I know to be true now that I didn't know a year ago?

Date:

# Day Twenty-Six

If you had to describe how you feel today as a color, what color would your feelings be and why?

Date:

# Day Twenty-Seven

Who is someone that always makes you smile and what is it about them that brings you joy?

# Day Twenty-Eight

You have 30 seconds to tell someone what you're passionate about - what will you say?

# Day Twenty-Nine

What are you most afraid of and why?

Date:

# Day Thirty

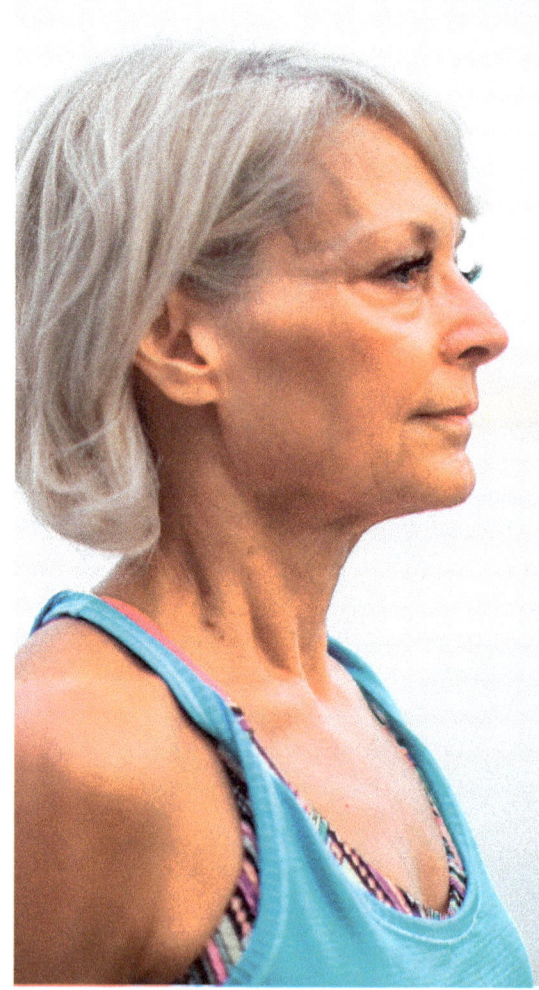

If you could go back in time and fix one mistake you made, which mistake would you fix?

Date:

# Day Thirty-One

What makes you feel cozy and safe?

# Day Thirty-Two

If I could make one promise to myself, it would be...

# Day Thirty-Three

What are three lies you often tell yourself? What three affirmations can you use to combat those lies?

# Day Thirty-Four

You're taking your inner child on a date today. What are you going to do?

Date:

# Day Thirty-Five

What is one smell that immediately transports you to a happy memory, and what is the memory?

Date:

# Day Thirty-Six

What are your core values? Are you living your life in accordance with them?

# Day Thirty-Seven

What do I need to let go of today??

# Day Thirty-Eight

How would you approach your work differently today if you weren't worried about the approval of others?

Date:

# Day Thirty-Nine

What makes your heart sing? When do you feel fully alive?

# Day Forty

If you could go back and tell your child self one thing, what would it be? How can you take this same thing with you now as an adult?

Date:

# Day Forty-One

This is something I really wish other people knew about me...

Date:

# Day Forty-Two

What's something you can do first thing in the morning to help you feel peaceful and grounded (maybe even before you open your eyes)?

Date:

# Day Forty-Three

Do you believe being happy is a good goal in life? Why or why not?

# Day Forty-Four

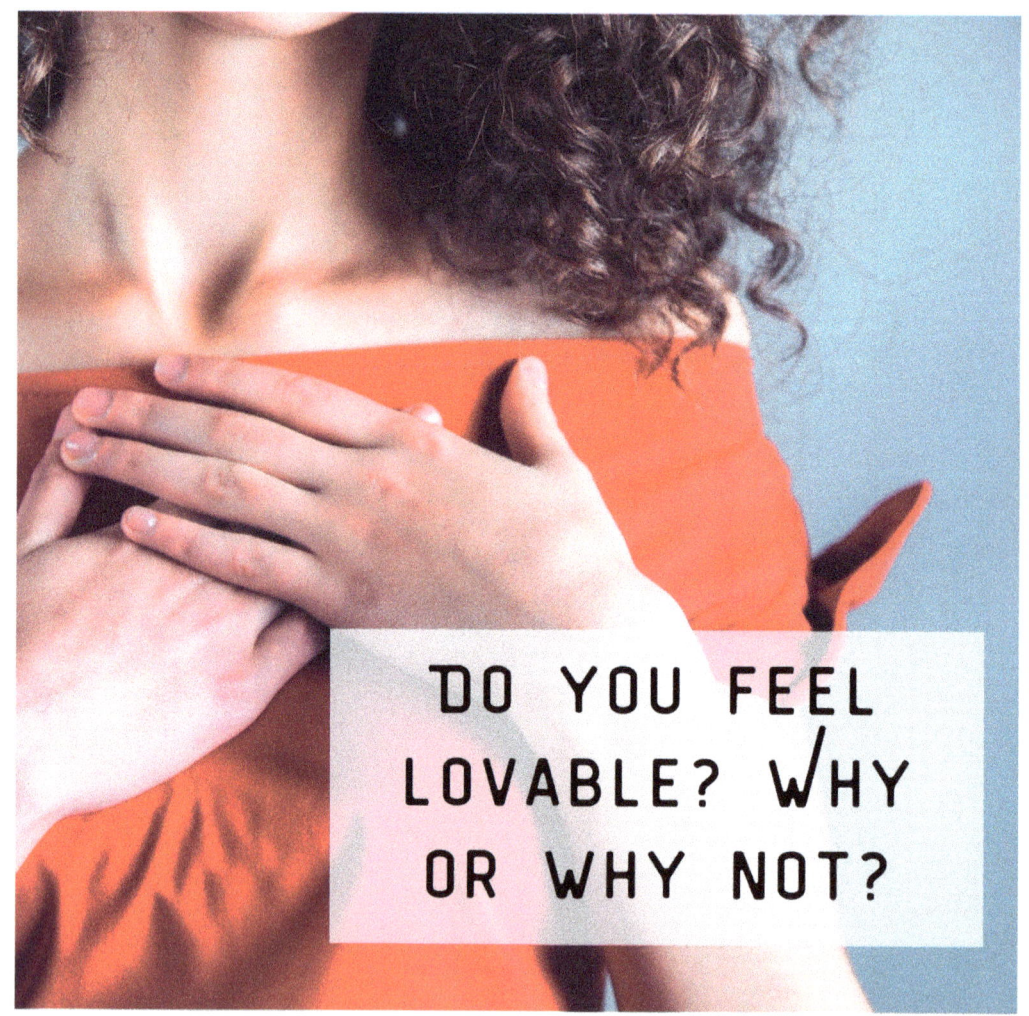

DO YOU FEEL LOVABLE? WHY OR WHY NOT?

Date:

# Day Forty-Five

Date:

# Day Forty-Six

What kind of person did you look up to when you were a child? What kind of person do you look up to now? What changed or stayed the same?

Date:

# Day Forty-Seven

When I really stop and pay attention to my heart, this is what I realize it needs...

Date:

# Day Forty-Eight

What's something you could do just for fun today?

# Day Forty-Nine

When you wake up in the morning, do you usually feel calm & peaceful, anxious & on high alert, or depressed & tired? Do you know why?

Date:

# Day Fifty